せがわ せつこ キルトの世界-Ⅲ

JAPANESE QUILT ART Ⅲ

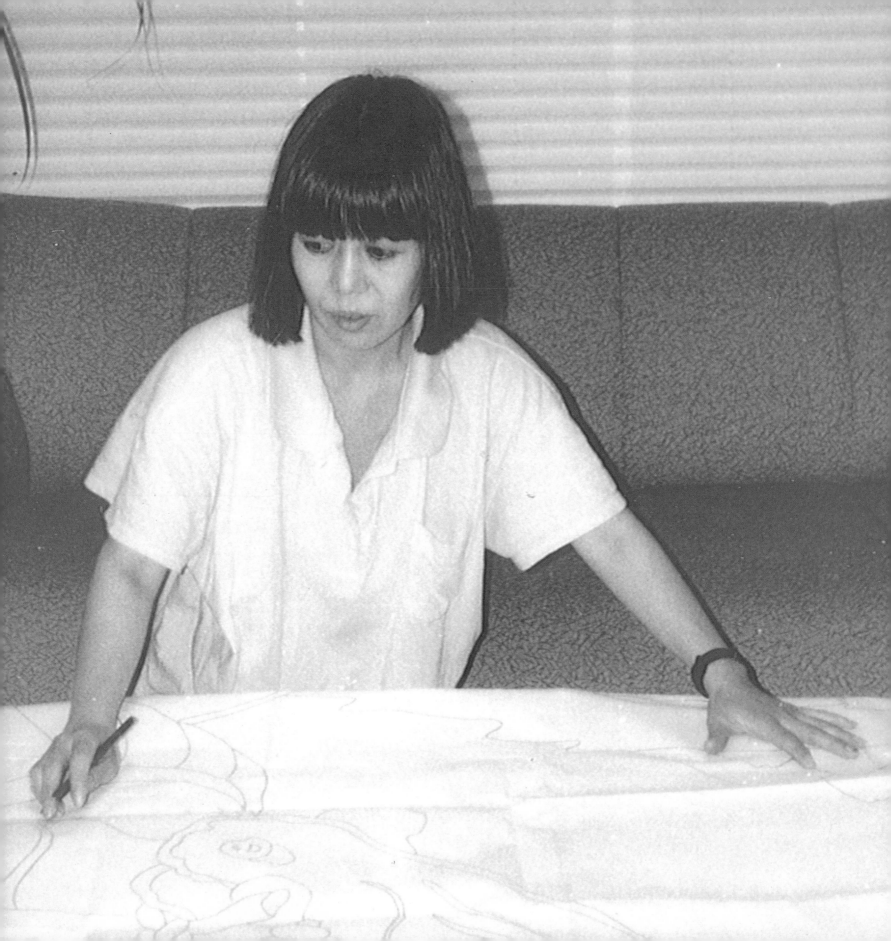

せがわ せつこ キルトの世界-Ⅲ

JAPANESE QUILT ART Ⅲ

by Setsuko Segawa

Published by Mitsumura Suiko Shoin

Japan

せがわせつこ著

光村推古書院刊

JAPANESE QUILT ART—Ⅲ

First Edition August 1989 by Mitsumura Suiko Shoin Co.,Ltd.
Fuyacho-dori Nijo Agaru, Nakagyo-ku, Kyoto 604 Japan
English Translation:Janice Brown & Michiko Takagi
Editor:Kinzo Honda (Mitsumura Suiko Shoin Co.,Ltd.)
© 1989 Setsuko Segawa   Printed in Japan

ISBN4-8381-0103-1

目　次
CONTENTS

はじめに ──────── せがわせつこ ──── 9
Preface   Setsuko Segawa

カラー図版
color plates

❶燃え木色に染まる ──────────── 13
Dyed burning red
Teinture rouge brûlante

❷宴 ─────────────────── 14
Banquet
Banquet

❸戦さよ終われ ──────────── 16
Put an end to war
Terminez la guerre

❹部 分 ─────────────── 17
detail

❺陽光を浴びて ──────────── 18
Bathing in sunlight
Bain de soleil

❻池に咲く ───────────── 19
Blooming in the pond
Épanouissement dans l'étang

❼蒼い花 ─────────────── 20
Blue flowers
Fleur bleue

❽部 分 ─────────────── 21
detail

❾谷間に咲く百合 ────────── 22
Lilies blooming in a ravine
Épanouissement des lis dans le ravin

❿秋 風 ─────────────── 23
Autumn wind
Vent d'automne

⓫香 光 ─────────────── 24
Fragrant light
Lumière aromatique

⓬獅子の戯れ ──────────── 26
Lion at play
Jeuz des lions

⓭部 分 ─────────────── 27
detail

⓮時代の狭間Ⅰ ──────────── 28
A moment in time I
Un moment du temps I

⓯時代の狭間Ⅱ ──────────── 29
A moment in time II
Un moment du temps II

⓰部 分 ─────────────── 30
detail

⓱朱 竹 ─────────────── 31
Red bamboo
Bambou rouge

⓲冬到来 ─────────────── 32
Advent of winter
Arrivée d'hiver

⓳部 分 ─────────────── 33
detail

⓴浮上の山Ⅰ ──────────── 34
Floating mountains I
Montagnes flottantes I

㉑浮上の山Ⅱ ──────────── 35
Floating mountains II
Montagnes flottantes II

㉒浮上の山Ⅲ ──────────── 36
Floating mountains III
Montagnes flottantes III

㉓浮上の山Ⅳ ──────────── 37
Floating mountains IV
Montagnes flottantes IV

㉔白彩の詩 ───────────── 38

Poem in white
Poème en blanche

㉕春の訪れ ——————— 39
Spring visit
Visite du printemps

㉖秋日和 I ——————— 40
Clear fall weather I
Temps clair en automne I

㉗部　分 ——————— 41
detail

㉘舞詩 I ——————— 42
Dance poem I
Poème de la danse I

㉙舞詩 II ——————— 43
Dance poem II
Poème de la danse II

㉚六ひょうたん ——————— 44
Six gourds
Six gourdes

㉛浮世絵美人 ——————— 45
Beauties of Ukiyoe Prints
Beautés du Ukiyoe

㉜勇　者 ——————— 46
Hero
Héros

㉝安息日 ——————— 47
Day of rest
Jour du repos

㉞秘境に咲いた花 ——————— 48
Flower blooming in a secret place
Épanouissement dans la place secretète

㉟部　分 ——————— 49
detail

㊱絡んだ紐 ——————— 50
Twisted strands
Cordes tordues

㊲秋日和 II ——————— 52
Clear fall weather II
Temps clair en automne II

㊳麦　秋 ——————— 53
Wheat harvest
Automne de blé

㊴冬景色 ——————— 54
Winter scene
Paysage d'hiver

㊵部　分 ——————— 55
detail

㊶湿地帯 ——————— 56
Swamp
Marais

㊷秋のプレリュード ——————— 58
Autumn prelude
Prélude de l'automne

㊸大空へ ——————— 59
Up to the sky
Monter au ciel

㊹ビルラッシュ I ——————— 60
Building boom I
Bâtiments impétueux I

㊺ビルラッシュ II ——————— 61
Building boom II
Bâtiments impétueux II

㊻緑の光 ——————— 62
Green reflection
Réflexion verte

㊼光を求めて ——————— 63
Seeking the light
À la recherche de la lumière

㊽分裂した異分子 ——————— 64
Diverse elements broken up
Éléments diverses scindés

㊾放　光 ——————— 65

Emmision of light
Émission de la lumière

50 露 ——————————————— 66
Dew
Rosée

51 未知との遭遇 ——————————— 67
Meeting the unknown
Rencontre de l'inconnu

52 或る日の記憶 ——————————— 68
Memory of a certain day
Mémoire d'un jour particulier

53 ひとりだけの劇 ——————————— 69
A play for one person only
Une piéce à l'acteur solitaire

54 放浪する分度器 ——————————— 70
Wandering Protractor
Rapporteur errant

55 一日だけの気紛れ ——————————— 71
Only one day's whim
Caprice d'un seul jour

56 雨に唄えば ——————————— 72
Singing in the rain
En chantant dans la pluie

57 部 分 ——————————————— 73
detail

58 乱気流 ——————————————— 74
Turbulence
Turbulence

59 光 ——————————————————— 75
Light
Lumière

60 紳士と淑女の出逢い ——————————— 76
When of ladies and gentlemen meet
Rencontre des Mesdames et Messieurs

61 風に揺れて ——————————— 77
Trembling in the wind

En tremblant au vent

62 漂 流 ——————————————— 78
Drifting
Flottement

63 戯 れ ——————————————— 79
Play
Jeu

64 愛のコラール ——————————— 80
Love chorale
Choral d'amour

65 部 分 ——————————————— 81
detail

66 スパニッシュファン ——————————— 82
Spanish fan
Éventail espagnol

67 幻想花 ——————————————— 84
Fantasy flower
Fleur de fantaisie

作品解説 ——————————————— 85
About the works ——————————— 89
制作順序 ——————————————— 93
Making the quilts

あとがき
制作協力

はじめに
PREFACE

せがわせつこ
Setsuko Segawa

冬の陽だまりに佇んでいる私の前を一枚の枯れ葉がよぎっていく——ひらひらと風に揺れ、宙に舞いあがる様は、まるで狂女が舞っているかと思えば、恋人につれなくされて嘆き悲しむかのようにも見え、また、人をあざけ笑うように舞い上がっていくようにも見える。

　こんなふうに季節が移り変わり、さまざまな出会いの中で、私も心の服を一枚ずつ脱いでいくのかもしれない。無意味に年を重ねて生きることの出来ない性格ゆえに、時々、考え込んでナーヴァスになり心のブラックホールに落ちてしまうが、また、すぐに光を求めて這いあがる。そんな時自分に、「お前はスチューピッド（愚か者）だ！穴でも掘って自分で自分を埋めてしまえ！」と言ってみる。この言葉の裏にはもろさもある。が、自分の中のもろさに勝ち、今までの体験も自分のアドバンテージにして生きてゆきたい。

　私には、私をキルトアーティストとして陰で応援してくれる家族がいて、友がいる。信頼できる生徒がいる。そして八年間逢えない娘達がいる。その娘達がひとりの女性として、大人としての考えを持ち再会できた時、私は、精一杯抱きしめてやるだろう。私の心の中に彼女達はいつも生きているのだから。きっと理解してくれるだろうと信じている。自己の心のバランスを保つためにいつでも軌道修正が出来る状態でいたいと思うし、自由な心で娘達を迎えたいと思っている。

　先日、空の色にみとれている私に車中検札の車掌が肩をポンポンとたたいた。私はめんどくさいなと思いながら切符を片手で出した。隣の座席の客が「何

が見えますか」と聞いたので、私は「ほら、あの空の色」と返事をした。すると隣の客は「これは台風が向かってますなあ」という。私が見ていたのは空の色。確かに台風の色だが想いが異なっていた。

　私はさまざまな想いをめぐらせながら頭の中で一枚の絵を描いていた。人には個々の物の見方、感じ方がある。確かに台風は自然を破滅させてしまう力があるが、台風の前の空模様は子供の頃から気にいっている。「あんな空が描けたらなぁー」と思いながら今日まで来ている。

　私の作品のベースは自然が写し出す色が教え、与えてくれる。作風が少しずつ変化しつつあるのは、物に対する感じ方、受け止め方が微妙に変化しつつあるからだと思う。現実にとどまることを知らない私の心理現象といえるだろう。

　日本の持つ自然美は常に私を刺激し、魅了しつづける。海外での展覧会の打合せをしていて日本に生まれて良かったと思う。自分の感じたものを自分なりにチョイスし、表現する自己の感受性をいつまでも持ち続けられればと思う。流れ星のように一瞬に消えるのでなく満天の星のひとつでいいから。

　私はコンクールに一発勝負するのは苦手だが、その分、いつもマイペースで進み続けたい。どうも性格にあわないようだ。

　海外から、私を訪ねて見えたり、ぜひ展覧会を、と言ってくれる。見たい方には、どんな遠くの国であっても物を創り出す心は通じていると思うので、海外のエキゼヴィションも今年から考えている。

As I bask in the winter sun, autumn leaves drift by me. Fluttering in the wind, they seem to dance about like mad women. Are they sighing sadly for their lovers, or are they laughing at someone?

So the seasons change, as do the many experiences of my life, stripping away the layers of my heart one by one. Since I am not the sort of person who can live a meaningless life, I sometimes feel uneasy and think dark thoughts. I fall into a black hole and have to crawl towards the light. At those times I say to myself, "Stupid! Why don't you dig a hole and bury yourself?!" There is of course some weakness behind these words. However, I want to overcome such weakness and turn the experiences I have had up until now to my advantage. At the same time, I do not want to lose my kind and gentle feelings for others.

As a quilt artist, I have been fortunate to have the support of my family, friends and students. There are also my daughters whom I have not seen for eight years. When we meet again, as women and adults, I will embrace them heartily. They are always in my thoughts. I feel certain they understand me. To preserve the sense of balance within myself I always want to be able to change the course of my life should I so desire. And so, I hope to meet my daughters in a spirit of freedom.

Recently, as I was gazing raptly at the color of the sky from a train window, the conductor tapped me on the shoulder to ask for my ticket. Feeling somewhat annoyed at this interruption, I handed it over. The person sitting next to me asked. "What were you looking at?" When I replied, "At the color of the sky," my fellow passenger said, "It's that color because a typhoon is approaching." Even though that was actually the case, my thoughts on looking at the sky had been quite different.

When I think my thoughts, my head becomes full of pictures. Each person has his own way of seeing and feeling things. Certainly typhoons have the power to destroy, but since childhood I have loved the patterns that appear in the sky just before a typhoon. To be able to capture that color in my art has long been my wish.

The colors revealed in nature are the basis of my work. The fact that my style continues somewhat to change is because I myself am always changing slightly in the way I feel about things and in the way I react to them. You could say that I don't know how to confine myself to reality; that is my psychological idiosyncrasy.

The natural beauty of Japan is my inspiration. I feel fortunate to be a Japanese who can make arrangements for exhibitions abroad. I hope I can continue to have the sensitivity to choose those things which I feel best expresses my thoughts and feelings. I would rather be one star among many than a shooting star that vanishes in an instant. Although I am a tough competitor, I always want to progress at my own pace. Somehow this seems not to suit my character.

I have often been visited by interested people from abroad and encouraged to have an overseas exhibition. Since I feel that the creative spirit of the artist can make itself understood in every part of the world, I would like to say to those who want to see my work that as of now I am thinking about an exhibition abroad.

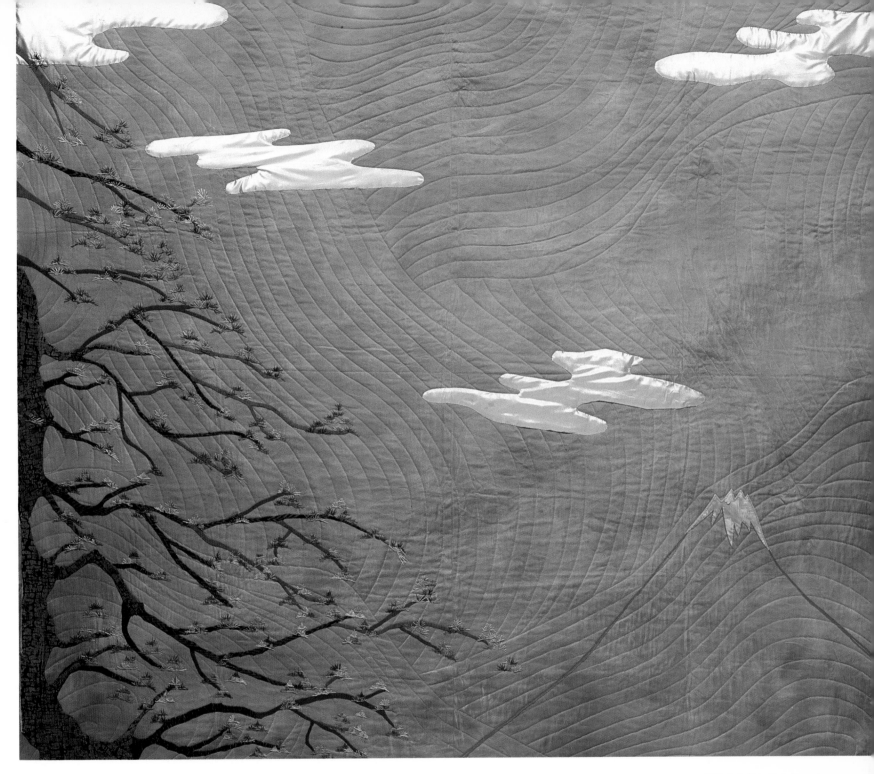

茜空に染まると

樹々は燃え木色となり

心は自己への未知数と浪漫を求め

旅へとかりたてられる──

❶燃え木色に染まる
Dyed burning red
Teinture rouge brûlante
1930×2200㎜

❷宴
Banquet
Banquet
2500×3140mm

❸戦さよ終われ
Put an end to war
Terminez la guerre
1980×1770mm

❹部分
detail

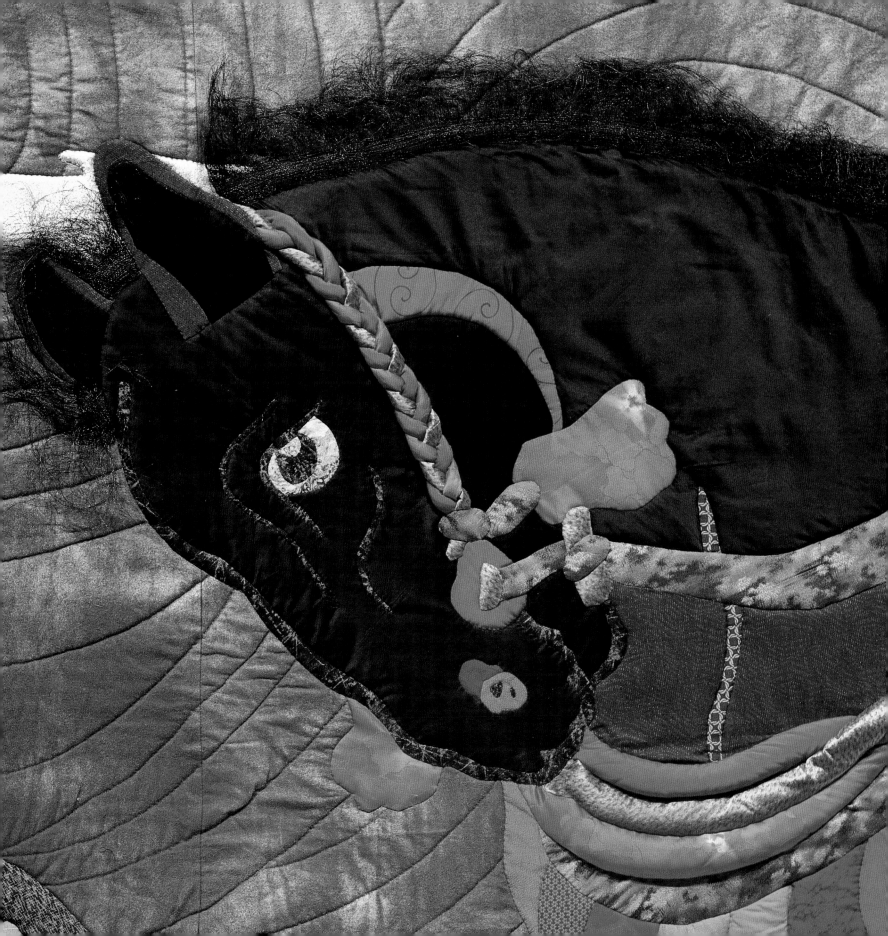

❺陽光を浴びて
Bathing in sunlight
Bain de soleil
1620×1060mm

18

❻池に咲く
Blooming in the pond
Épanouissement dans
l'étang
1200×945㎜

19

❼蒼い花
Blue flowers
Fleur bleue
1605×1905mm

20

❽部分
detail

❾谷間に咲く百合
Lilies blooming in a ravine
Épanouissement des lis dans le ravin
1560×1880mm

❿秋　風
Autumn wind
Vent d'automne
1550×1820mm

❶香　光
Fragrant light
Lumière aromatique
865×1970mm

❷獅子の戯れ
Lion at play
Jeuz des lions
1685×1490mm

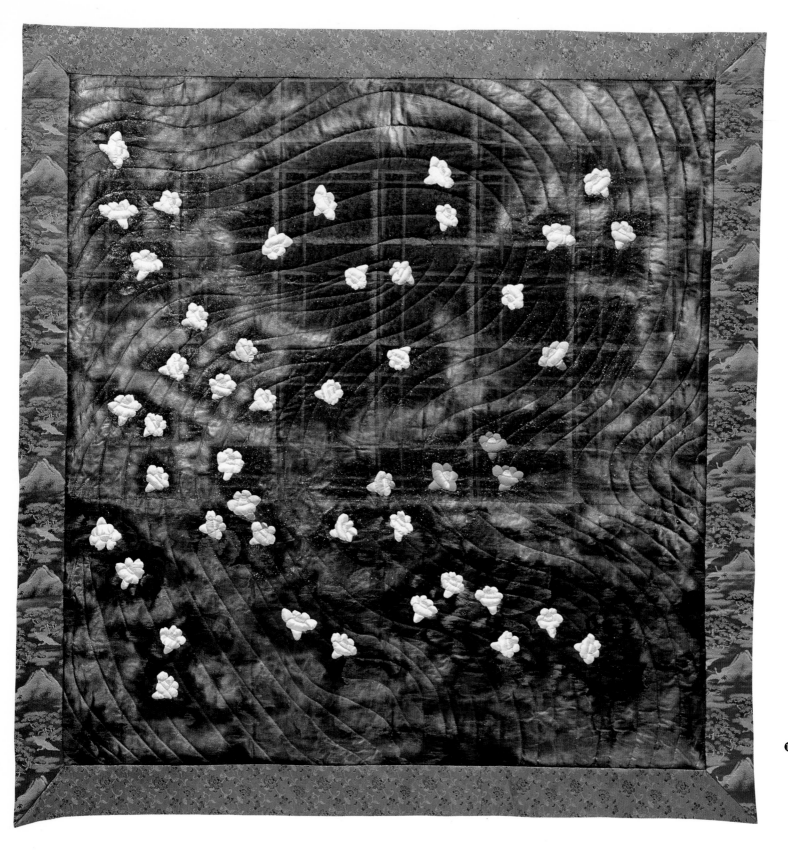

⓮時代の狭間 I
A moment in
time I
Un moment du
temps I
1760×1720mm

28

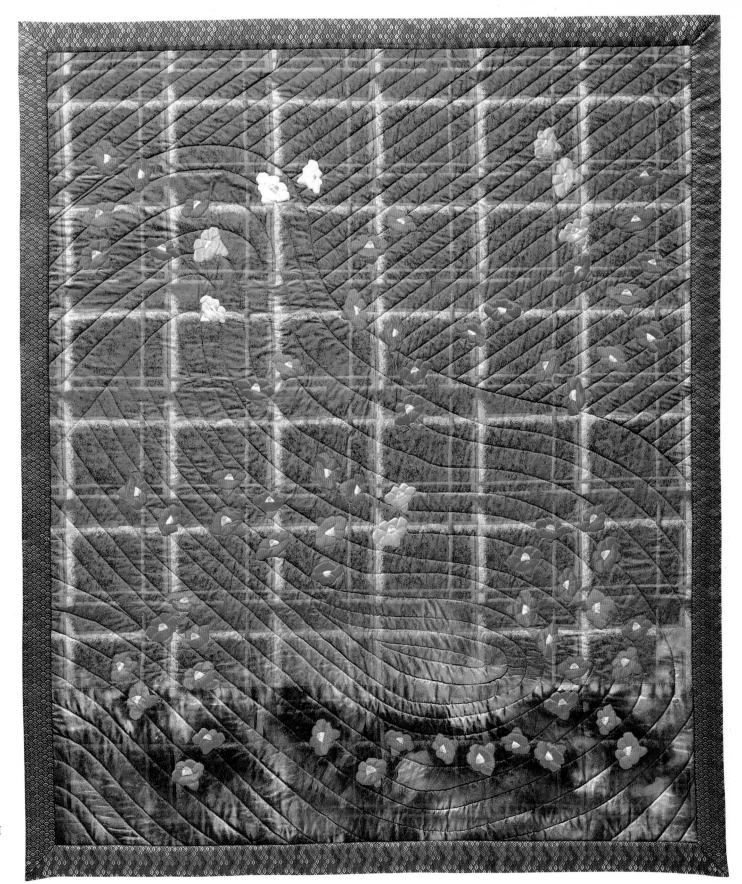

⓯時代の狭間Ⅱ

A moment in time Ⅱ

Un moment du
temps Ⅱ

1780×1510mm

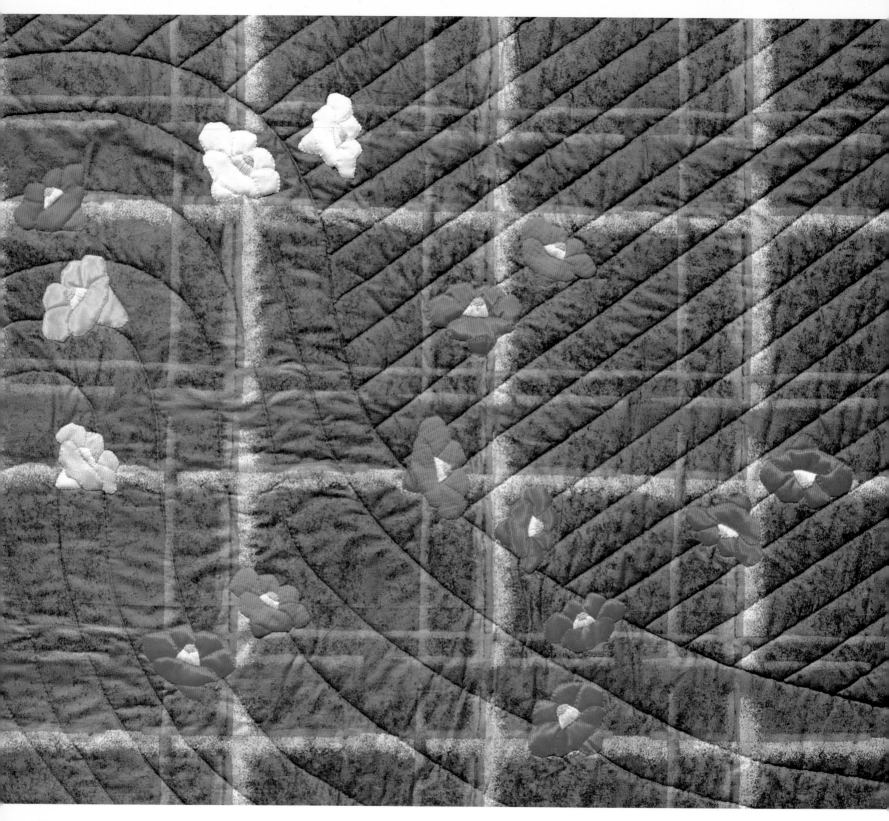

⓰部分(時代の狭間Ⅱ)
detail

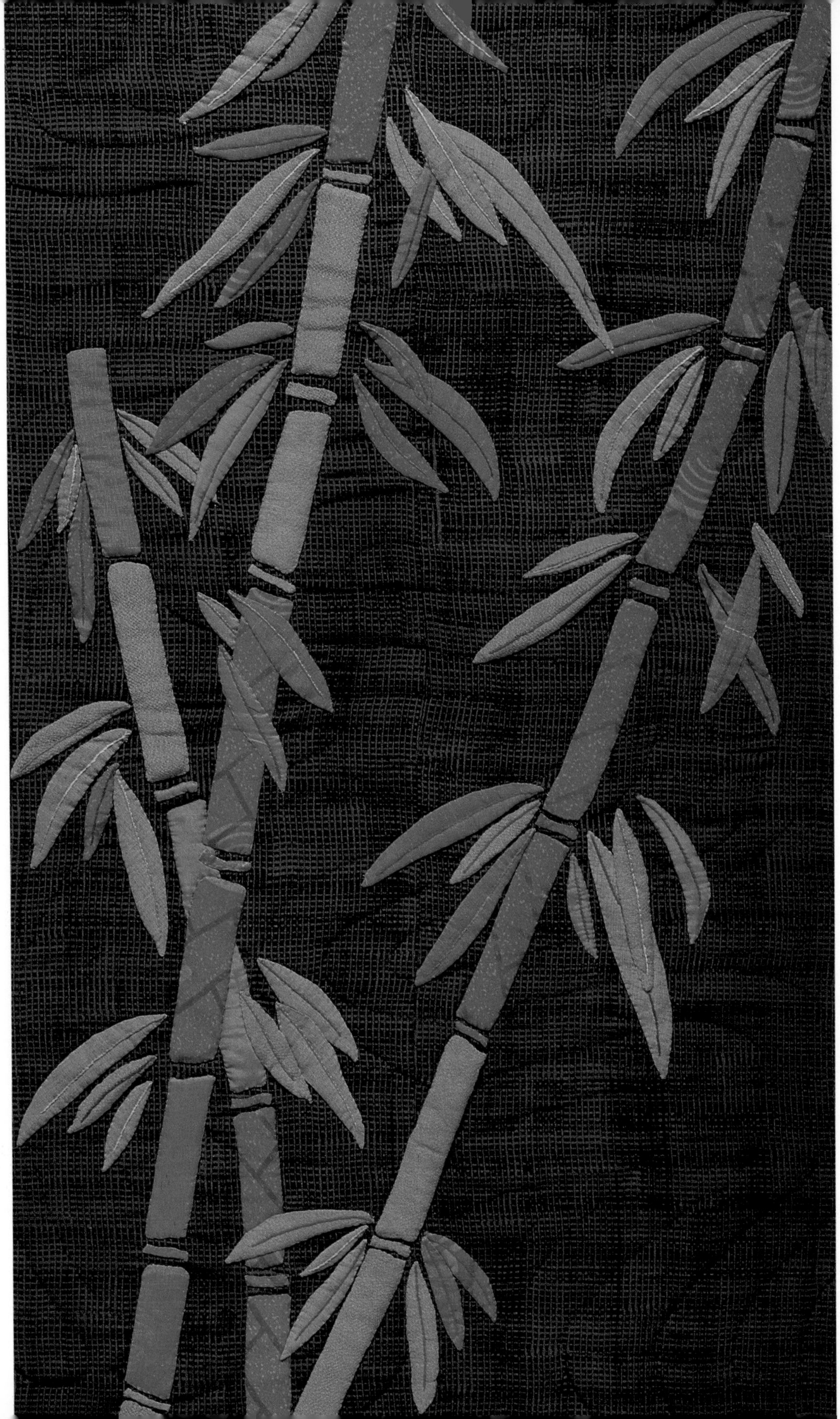

⓱朱　竹
Red bamboo
Bambou rouge
1200×745㎜

❽冬到来
Advent of winte
Arrivée d'hiver
2370×1980mm

❾部分
detail

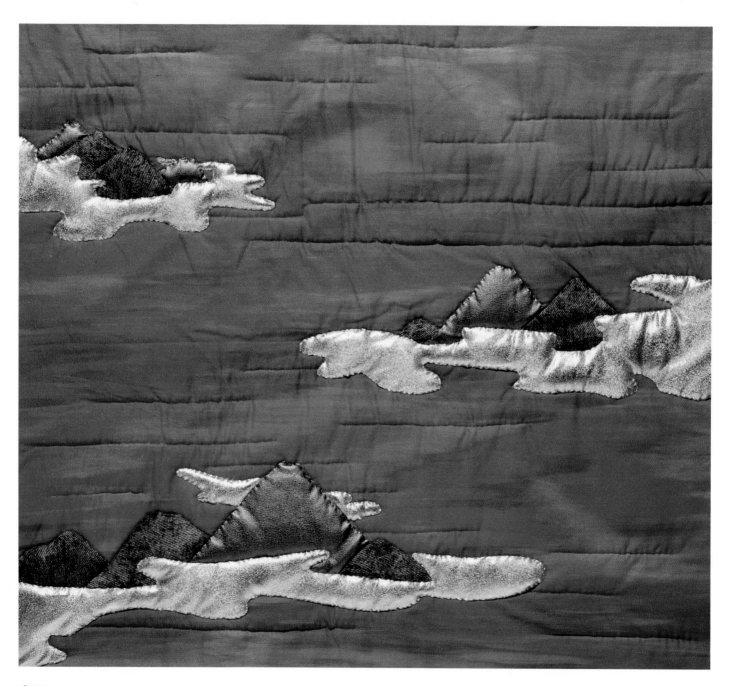

❷⓪浮上の山 I
Floating mountains I
Montagnes flottantes I
480×540㎜

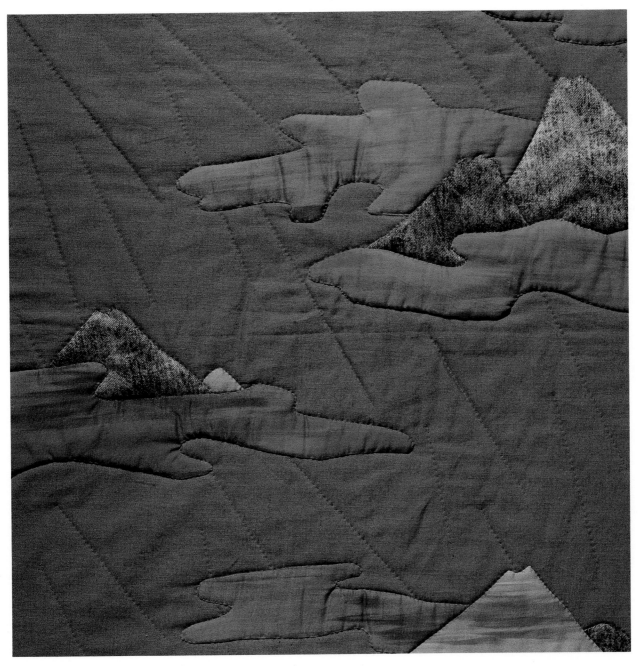

㉑浮上の山II
Floating mountains II
Montagnes flottantes II
540×540mm

㉒浮上の山Ⅲ

Floating mountains Ⅲ

Montagnes flottantes Ⅲ

460×500㎜

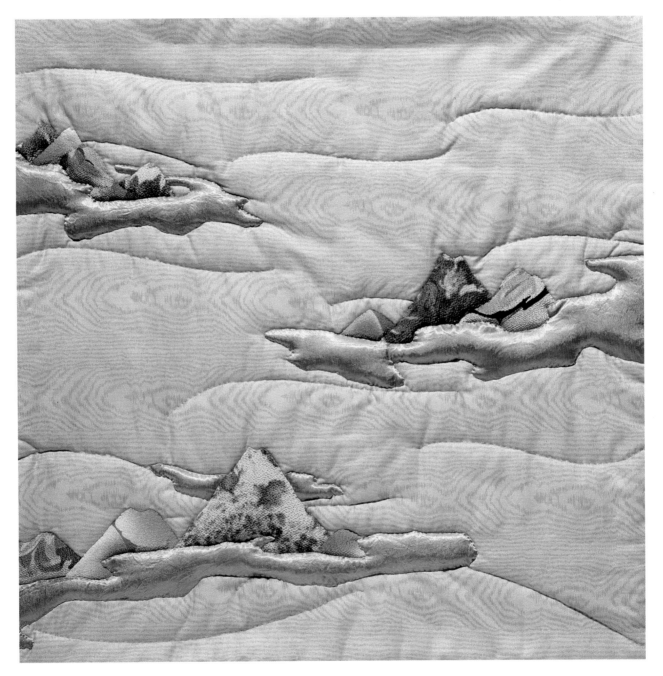

㉓浮上の山Ⅳ
Floating mountains Ⅳ
Montagnes flottantes Ⅳ
510×525mm

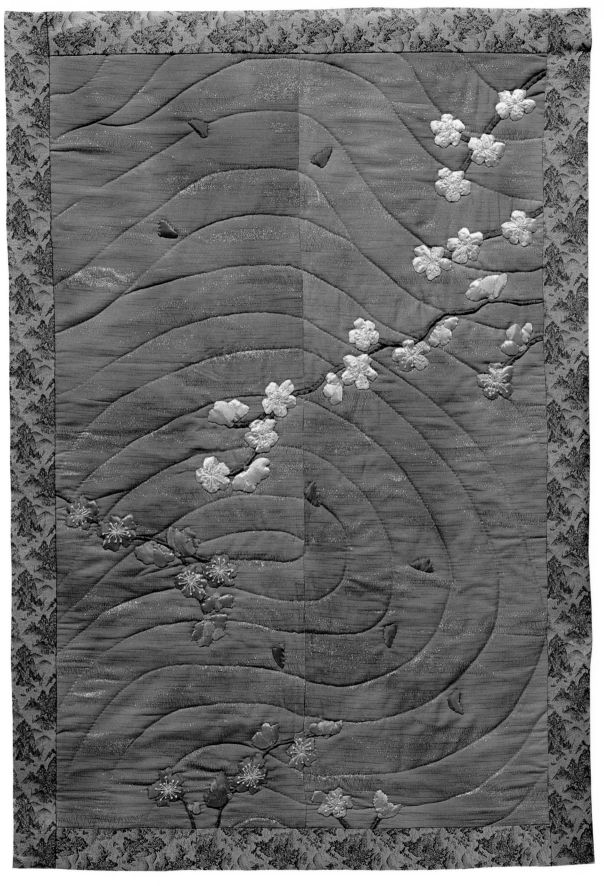

㉕春の訪れ
Spring visit
Visite du printemps
1170×820mm

㉔白彩の詩
Poem in white
Poème en blanche
1950×2150mm

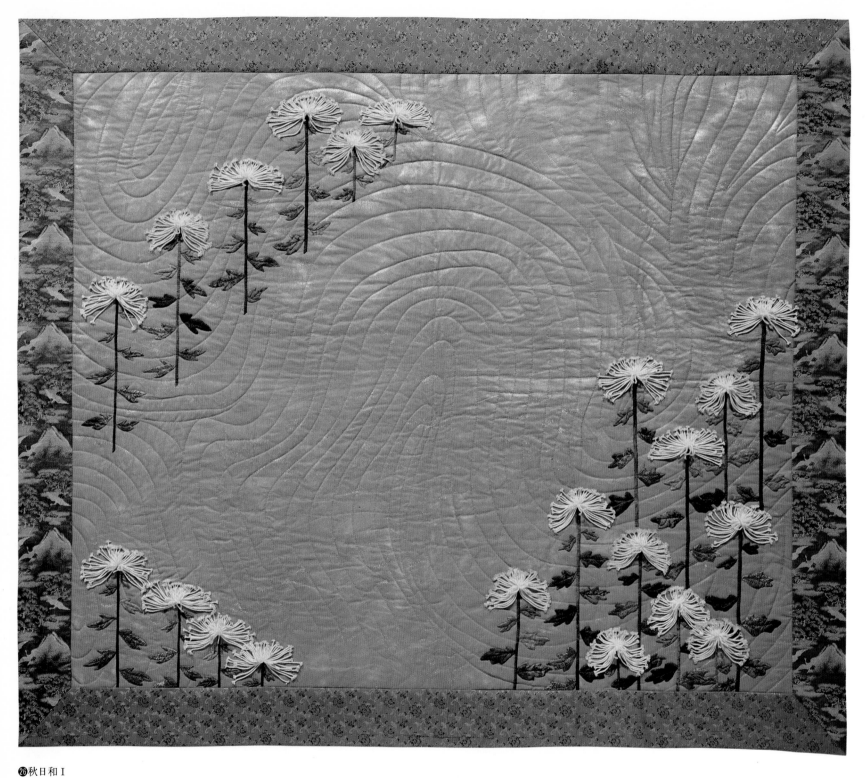

㉖秋日和 I

Clear fall weather I

Temps clair en automne I

1740×2040mm

27 部分
detail

㉘舞　詩Ⅰ

Dance poem Ⅰ

Poème de la danse Ⅰ

1950×2200mm

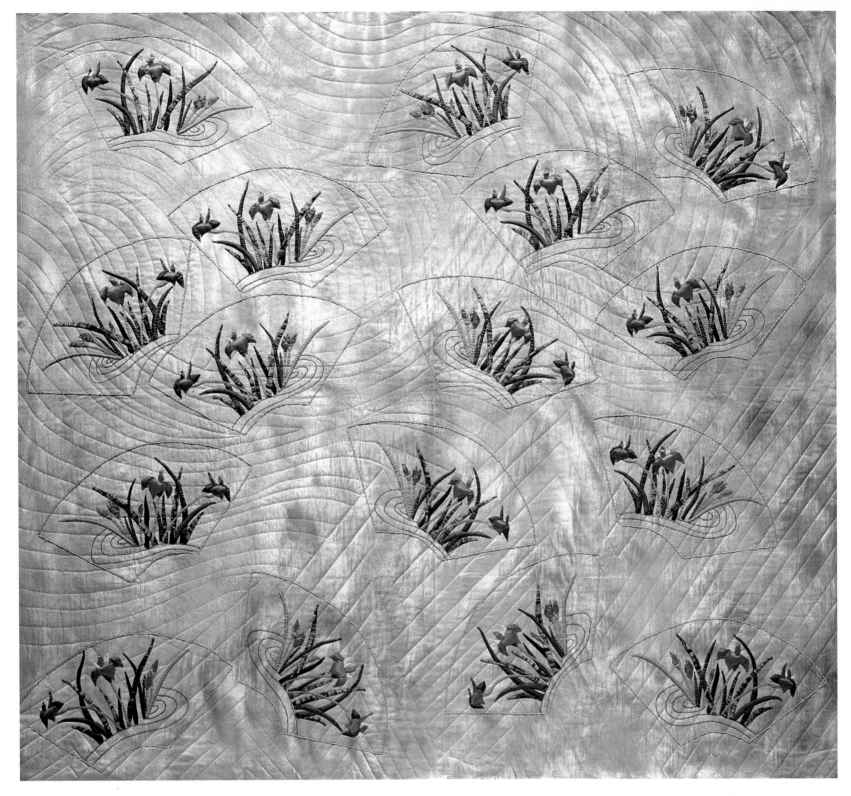

㉙舞　詩II
Dance poem II
Poème de la danse II
1950×2200mm

㉚六ひょうたん
Six gourds
Six gourdes
1595×1015mm

㉜勇　者
Hero
Héros
1780×1340mm

㉝安息日
Day of rest
Jour du repos
2050×1435mm

❸❹秘境に咲いた花

Flower blooming in a secret place

Épanouissement dans la place secretète

1615×1900mm

❸❺部分
detail

㊱絡んだ紐
Twisted strands
Cordes tordues
2210×2180mm

51

㊲秋日和 II
Clear fall weather II
Temps clair en automne II
1655×1205mm

㊲麦 秋
Wheat harvest
Automne de blé
770×525mm

❸❾冬景色
Winter scene
paysage d'hiver
1880×860mm

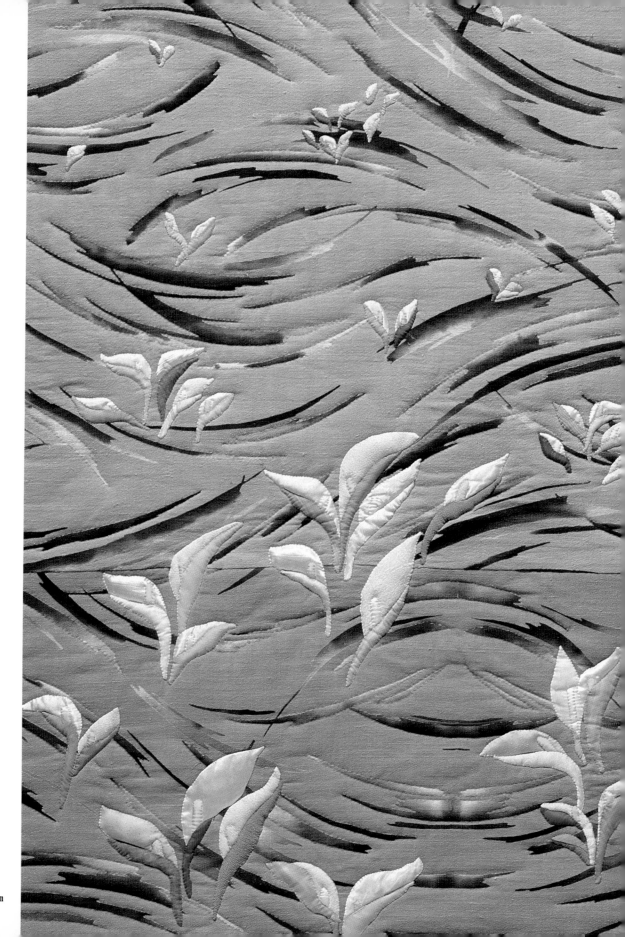

❹湿地帯
Swamp
Marais
1290×1580mm

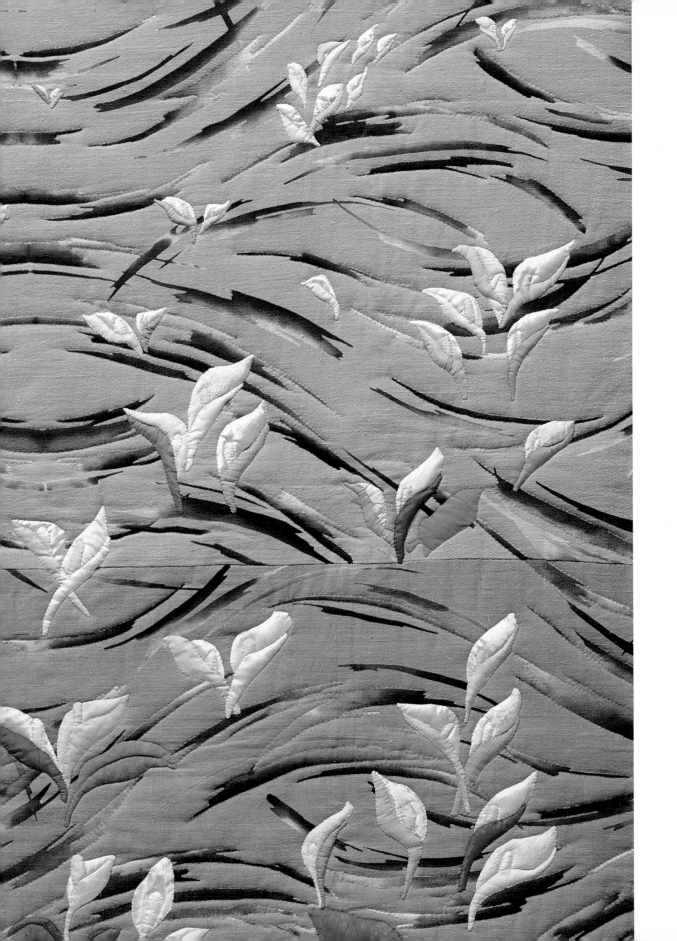

街路樹は
セピアに彩づきはじめ
私は風に吹かれて
流されて舞い上がる
風はさりげなく
季節の分水嶺を
越えてゆく

❹秋のプレリュード
Autumn prelude
Prélude de l'automne
680×510㎜

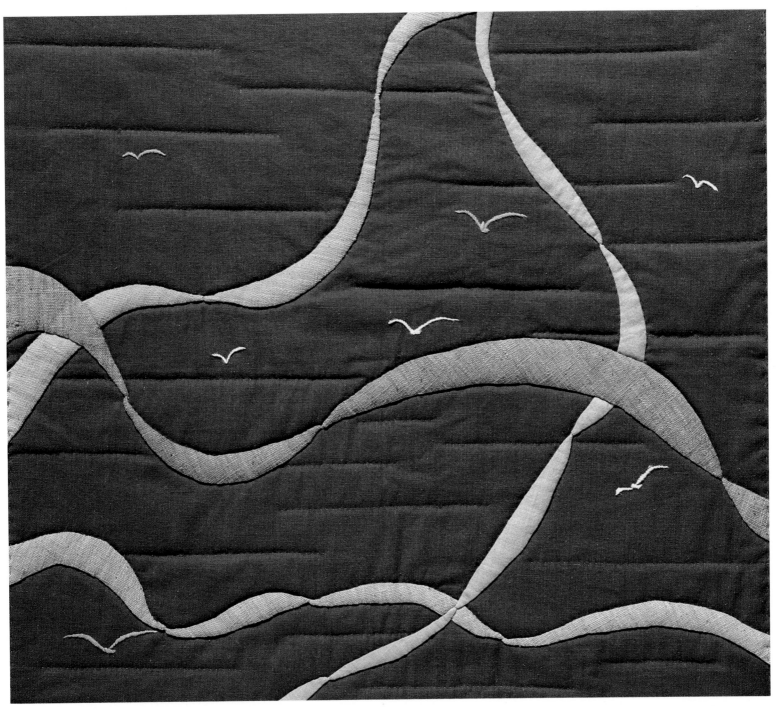

⑬大空へ
Up to the sky
Monter au ciel
480×540mm

⑭ビルラッシュ I
Building boom I
Bâtiments
impétueux
1825×2210mm

㊺ビルラッシュII
Building boom II
Bâtiments impétueux II
1710×1910mm

㊻緑の光
Green reflection
Reflexion verte
520×720mm

㊼光を求めて
Seeking the light
À la recherche de la lumière
700×985mm

❹❽分裂した異分子
Diverse elements broken up
Éléments diverses scindés
920×1330mm

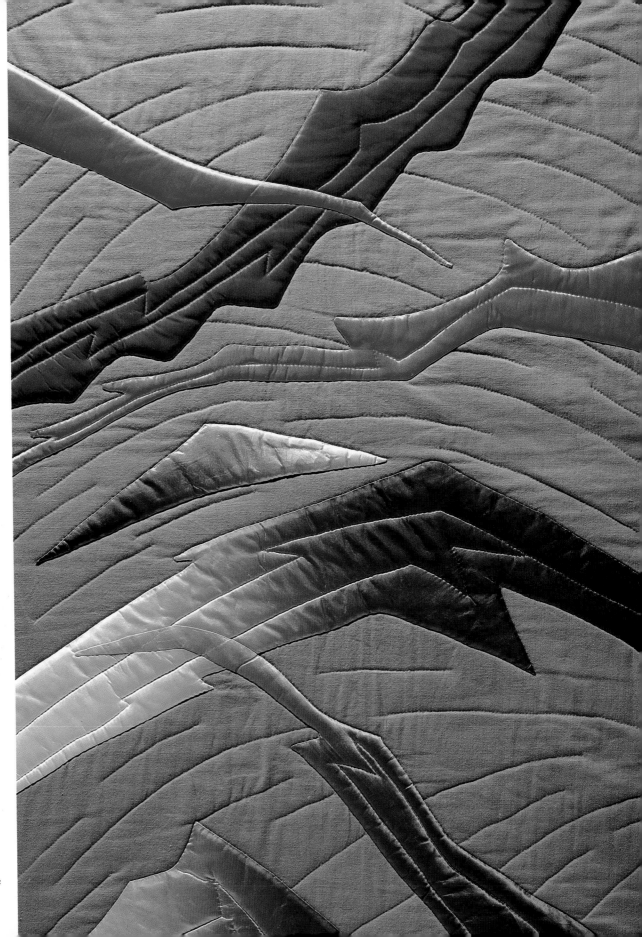

子供達の手の中を
そっと覗き込むと
光のメッセンジャーがいた
悲しいほど青く淡い光を放つ螢
あれから八年もの歳月が
流れてしまった

❹放 光
Emmision of light
Émission de la lumière
965×700㎜

(50)露
Dew
Rosée
715×515mm

(51)未知との遭遇
Meeting the unknown
Rencontre de l'inconnu
520×530mm

㊾或る日の記憶

Memory of a certain day
Mémoire d'un jour particulier
460×500mm

娘は月を取ってほしいという
困った私は洗面器を探しに行き、水を入れ
月を見せてやろうとしたが
娘はぐっすりと眠ってしまってた

㊾ひとりだけの劇
A play for one person only
Une piéce á l'acteur solitaire
520×540mm

㊿放浪する分度器
Wandering protractor
Rapporteur errant
520×780mm

❺一日だけの気紛れ
Only one day's whim
Caprice d'un seul jour
480×510mm

❺❻雨に唄えば
Singing in the rain
En chantant dans la pluie
2015×1460㎜

❸乱気流
Turbulence
Turbulence
510×500mm

㊉光
Light
Lumière
2020×1480mm

❻⓪紳士と淑女の出逢い
The meeting of ladies and gentlman
Rencontre de monsieur et madame
2020×1480㎜

❻風に揺れて
Trembling in the wind
En tremblantau vent
2000×1450㎜

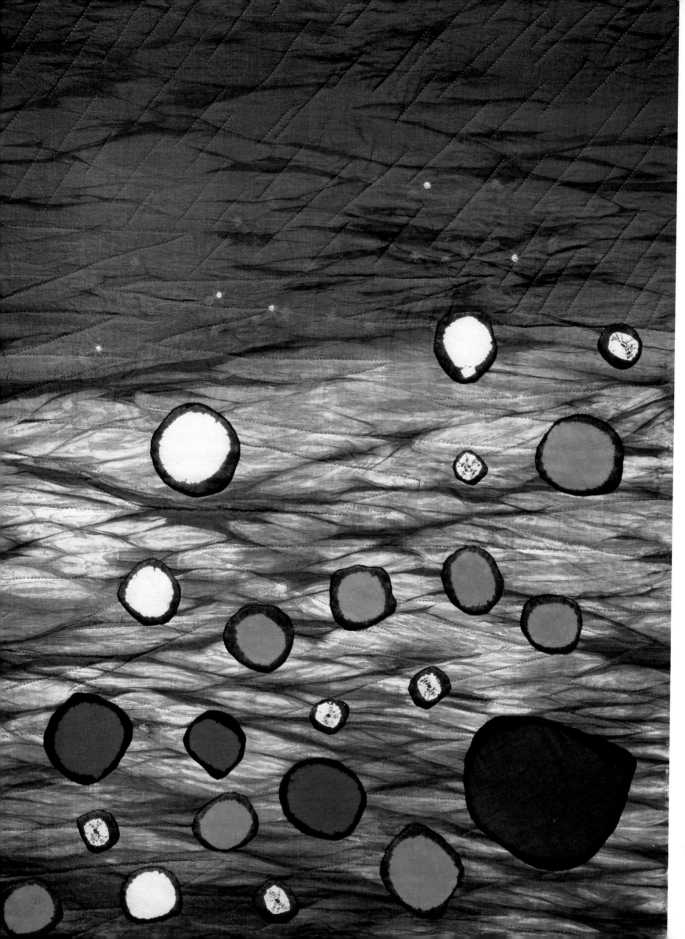

㉒漂　流
Drifting
Flottement
1260×940㎜

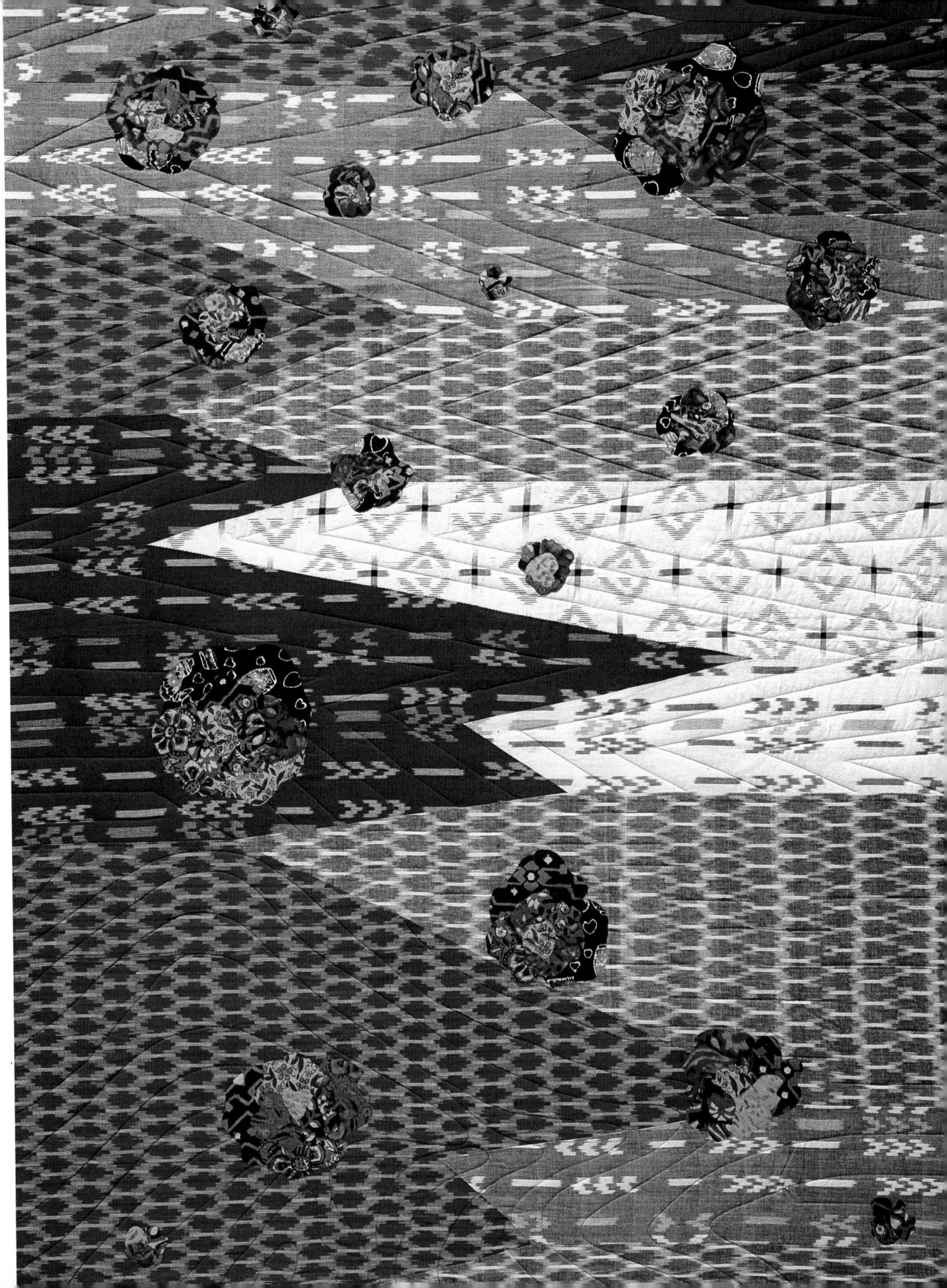

(63)戯　れ
play
Jeu
2000×1485mm

64 愛のコラール
Love chorale
Choral d'amour
685×495mm

65 部分
detail

㊏スパニッシュファン
Spanish fan
Éventail espagnol
1220×1910mm

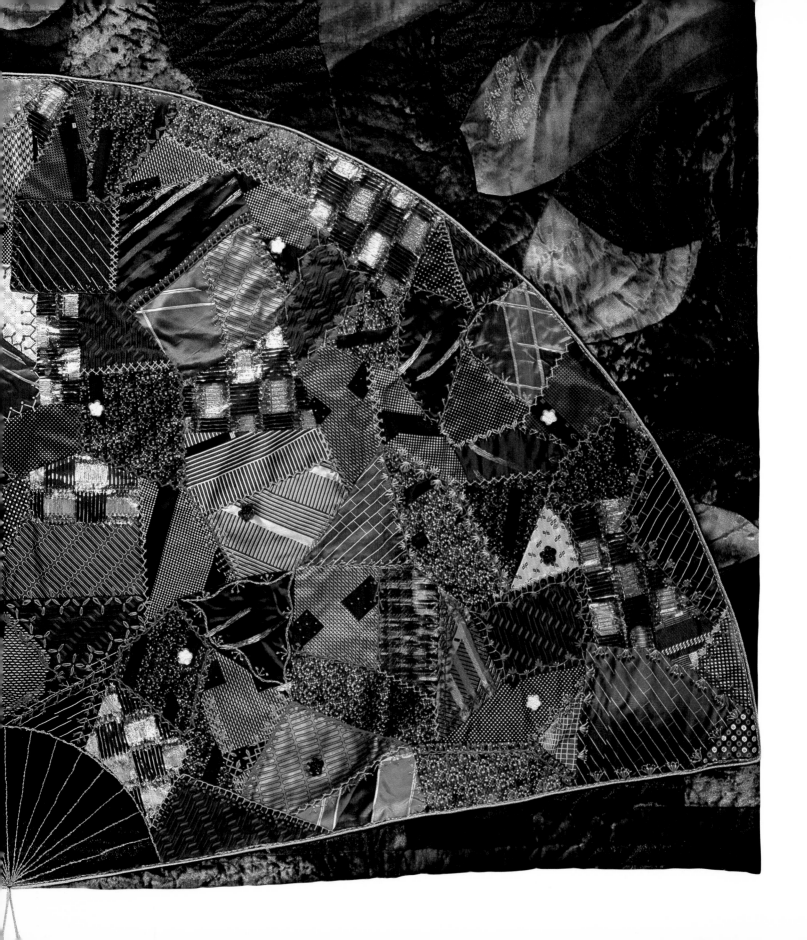

❻❼幻想花
Fantasy flower
Fleur de fantaisie
880×500mm

作 品 解 説

❶燃え木色に染まる

　すべての景色が燃え木色に染まる。未知の自然の色に染まってゆく様を、何人の人が感動する心の余裕を持っているだろうか。私の心はこの瞬間的な色の美しさに魅了され、動へとかりたてられる。

　ベースは白いシーチング。キルトをした上にアクリルカラーをかけ、アップリケと刺繍で現した。

❷宴

　陽光を浴び、優雅に舞う鶴。日本の古典的な色を背景に、鶴を描きたいと思った。

　ベースは白のシーチング。アクリルカラーで何色もの色を重ねて染め、すすきはサマーヤーン、花の部分と鶴はアップリケ、松は刺繍をしてみた。

❸❹戦さよ終われ

　戦いが早く終わってほしいと願うのは決して人間だけとは限らないと思う。動物にしても、そう願っているであろう。

　明るい光のきざしを光沢のある布を使い雲に現した。馬のたてがみは麻布をほぐし、色をかけた。

❺陽光を浴びて

　新しい年の幕開け。新春のひきしまった気持ちで初光を浴びて鶴が舞い上がる様子を表現した。

❻池に咲く

　池に咲く花しょうぶ。日本の初夏を代表する花。

　光で水面が光って見える様子はぼかしのサテンを使用し、キルトラインで動きを現した。

❼❽蒼い花

　すがすがしい朝もやの中に咲きほこる蒼色の牡丹の花を描いた。

　素材は着物地で、サテンを使用し、花芯は刺繍。

❾谷間に咲く百合

　深い山の谷あいに咲く百合。余りの美しさに手折ってみたくなるほど。崖の上に咲く山百合は、日本の自然の美しさを私に教えてくれる。

❿秋風

　私はなぜか紫色の花が好きだ。心が休まる。自然の中に咲く花を見ているせいであろう。庭先の糸すきの間から咲いている桔梗の花を見ていると、私に限らず、誰しもが秋の気配を感じるだろう。

⓫香光

　日本の古典美の花である牡丹は、日本の代表的な絵画にもよく現され、〝立てば芍薬、座れば牡丹、歩く姿は百合の花〟といわれる程、優雅な花姿である。特に白い牡丹は私の心をひきしめてくれる。

⓬⓭獅子の戯れ

　紺の綿布がベースで全体をリバースアップリケとアップリケでまとめた。

⓮時代の狭間Ⅰ　⓯⓰時代の狭間Ⅱ

　渦巻く時の流れ、昭和から平成へ、変わりつつあった瞬間を椿の花で動きを表現した。平和な時が続きますように願う心は世界中の人々が同じであろう。

⓱朱竹

　日本で竹は梅、松、蘭と共に四友といわれるひとつであり、おめでたいものとされ特に朱竹は祝い事にも使われる。

　ベースは着物生地、アップリケの部分は羽織、又はその裏、チリメンなどを使用。

⓲⓳冬到来

　冬木立をベースに鶴が飛び立つ。寒々とした大海原を越えている様を描いた。

　ベースは着物地、羽織地などをピーシングしてキ

ルトをし、冬木立はムラ染めにした布を使用。

⑳㉑㉒㉓浮上の山

はるか彼方に見える雲海に浮かぶ山々。或る時は金色に又、燃えるような赤に染まったり、どんよりとした空に覆われたり、又或る時は、空の景色によって変わってゆく。自然の持つ色は、とても言葉で一口にしては現せそうもない。

㉔白彩の詩

春に咲き誇る花はパレットの上にのせた絵具のようにカラフルだが、白木蓮は、品の良い白の美しさを持ち、日本の伝統的な絵画のテーマにもいくつかあげられているほどだ。私はいつかこの白木蓮を絵具で表現したいと思っている。

㉕春の訪れ

あざやかな桜の色ではないが、うすずみ色に変わってゆく花びら。春の終わりを惜しんで散る様は私の心の中にいつまでも残っている。

㉖㉗秋日和Ⅰ

秋の香りといえば、日本では、菊。丹精こめられた菊が各地で展示される。私もよく、スケッチに行ったり自分なりに菊づくりを楽しんだ頃がある。秋の夕焼けに咲き誇る菊を現した。

ベースは赤のシーチング。キルトしたあとにアクリルカラーをかけ、アップリケした。菊の花は綿コードを使用。

㉘舞詩Ⅰ　㉙舞詩Ⅱ

古典的な色をベースに『キルトの世界Ⅱ』でも表現した花と扇面図。

㉚六ひょうたん

六ひょうたんは日本では無病息災といわれ縁起物とされている。

ベースは風呂敷地、ひょうたんの部分は着物地を使用。

㉛浮世絵美人

着物生地のピーシングした上にキルトをして浮世絵のハンカチをかるた風においてみた。

㉜勇　者

五月の端午の節句には、武者人形を飾ったり、かしわもちを供える。男の子が元気でたくましく育つようにと昔からの願いである。

ベースはダンガリー、その上にアップリケして、ひげは岩絵具を使用、フレームは、インディゴの持つ風合いを生かしてみた。

㉝安息日

戦さの合間に水汲みに行く武士の姿は戦さも忘れたように思える。

ベースは夏の呂の帯地にキルトをして色をかけ武士の姿は着物地でアップリケした。

㉞㉟秘境に咲いた花

湿地帯の奥深く咲く花。

黒い布をベースに色をかけ、アップリケをして、湿地帯のイメージをガーゼに染めたり、カーテン地を染めて糸をぬいて上から縫い付けた。

㊱絡んだ紐

『キルトの世界Ⅱ』の〝放つ、捻転〟の作品のシリーズ。

布によって、色によって異なって見えることに注目してほしい。グレーのベースは着物地。ピースワークと一部がアップリケのミックスの技法。

㊲秋日和Ⅱ

のどかな秋風が吹く中で白菊が咲き香る様子。

ベースはピースワークした上にガーゼを染めて、一本ずつぬきとり、色を重ねた上に菊をアップリケした。

㊳麦　秋

すすきが秋風にそよぐ様を現した。

キルトのラインはあくまでも脇役。すすきのイメージをこわさぬようキルトラインを入れる穂の部分は、刺繍である。

㊴㊵冬景色

ベースは着物生地をピースワークして、上から、松、鶴、すいせんなどはアップリケ。

㊶湿地帯

沼地の奥深く咲く、水芭蕉を描いた。

ベースはプリント柄をそのまま使用し、キルトして花をアップリケした。

㊷秋のプレリュード

高原の秋は一足早く訪れ、すすきも草花も秋のデモンストレーションをするかのように、初秋の風の中でなびいている。ロッジの窓から見る景色も又、心を感傷的にさせる。

㊸大空へ

空高く舞い上がる鳥に私はいつもあこがれる。自分も翼がほしいからかもしれない。鳥は、私の永遠のテーマのひとつである。

㊹ビルラッシュⅠ

気付かないうちに次々とビルが立ち並ぶ。今日も又、ひとつ、一体どれだけの人達があのビルの中にいるのだろうと思う。

ビルの部分はウール系、ツィード、ジャージィなど紳士服の残り布を使用。窓はエクセーヌを使用してみた。

㊺ビルラッシュⅡ

ビル街にイルミネーションがつくと、空は自然のもつ色と人工的な光がミックスされた色となる。

ベースはサテン地を染め、ビルの部分はすべて紳士用のネクタイの裏と表を使用。窓の部分はネクタイの裏地、又、ネクタイの一部分を使用。

㊻緑の光

光が放される瞬間、光にもさまざまな色があると思う。自然の樹木が光を放つときはもしかすると緑色かもしれない。

キルトラインはより光を強調したかったので、長短の直線を組合せた。ベースは草木染めの麻、緑色の部分はすべてサテン地を使用。

㊼光を求めて

自然の草花のほとんどは陽の光の方へ向こうとしている。それは、人間、動物、植物も同じだ。光を求めて生きているからだと思う。

㊽分裂した異分子

素材は麻と綿、混合地、ベースはカラーヤーンでキルトし、絵具をかけた。

㊾放　光

稲光りのように光が流れる。すべての色がミックスされる。

素材は麻と綿の混合地。光の部分はすべてサテン地を使用。

㊿露

雨上がりの草花は緑色が美しい。その葉先に溜まった露は光を浴び、まるで真珠のようだ。

51未知との遭遇

今までに出会った事がない何かに出会う時、人の心は動揺し、不安と期待でいっぱいになる。

52或る日の記憶

人の記憶はコンピューターにインプットさせたようにはいかない。私の記憶もそうだ。すべてを明確におぼえている部分、又、おもむろにしか記憶がない部分、とぎれ、とぎれになって記憶している所などさまざまだ。心と脳の部分を現した。

53ひとりだけの劇

大道芸人の彼女は必死で劇を演じる。だれも振り向かない。しかし、だれかが振り向いて見てくれる

かもしれない。未来へのステージに備えて今日も又、一人だけの劇を演じる。

　ベースは麻と綿の混合地、髪の部分はビニールレザー、目と鼻と口はプリント柄を使用、顔の輪郭はキルトラインだけで表現した。

❺❹放浪する分度器

　私の分度器はどこにいったのだろう。又、今日もさがし求める。或る日、一か所から、たくさんの分度器が見つかる。

❺❺一日だけの気紛れ

　私は時々、気紛れで行動してしまう。ストレスが蓄積されると、気紛れに行動してみたくなる。一日だけの気紛れで又、現実に戻って行く。私のストレス解消法かもしれない。

❺❻❺❼雨に唄えば

　ジャズに〝雨に唄えば〟という名曲がある。軽やかなミュージカル。小さい頃、雨の中で傘と水たまりで遊んだ頃を思い出す。

❺❽乱気流

　一瞬、エアーポケットに落ちる。すべての人が動揺し、そしてざわめきが起こる。

　ベースは麻と綿の混合地。トップはサテンとビニールレザー、プリント柄を使用。

❺❾光

　夕暮れの中に突然の光―― 一瞬、何が起こったのだろう――。

　ベースはカラーシーチング。光の部分はビニールレザーの光沢のあるものを使用した。

❻⓪紳士と淑女の出逢い

　紳士と淑女の出逢いを帽子で描いた。

　ベースはカラーシーチング。キルトした上に帽子はアップリケした。

❻❶風に揺れて

　緑の風に柳が揺れる。

　ベースはカラーシーチング。柳はソフトデニム使用。

❻❷漂　流

　嵐に出会って人々が救いを求めている様。

　インディゴに染めた布の上に別のインディゴに染めた一部分をおき、キルトする。

❻❸戯　れ

　私の作品には、花を描いたものが多い。花を見ていると心が和みその美しさに時々、時間を忘れてしまうようだ。花は私に季節を感じさせ、美しさをも分けてくれる。そんな花の戯れをこんなふうに表現してみた。

❻❹❻❺愛のコラール

　花には蝶が、蝶には花が必要である。それは、人間社会の男と女と同じかも知れない。彼らがかもし出す愛の讃歌。

　花芯の部分は刺繡。

❻❻スパニッシュ・ファン

　きらびやかで情熱的なスペインの思い出。スペインの民族舞踊フラメンコ。私の記憶に残るスパニッシュ・ファンをクレイジーキルトにまとめてみた。

❻❼幻想花

　幻の花。夢の中でしか見たことがない花。

　素材はベースの布。洋服の裏地をチキンワイヤーに入れ、裏からまつりつける。

About the works

❶ Dyed burning red

Everything in this scene is dyed burning red. No doubt many people have the capacity to be moved by the unknown colors of nature. Colors seen in an instant fascinate and inspire me with their beauty.

The base is white sheeting. I have applied acrylic color to the quilt and then appliqué and embroidery.

❷ Banquet

A crane dances elegantly in the sun. I wanted to depict the crane against a background of classical Japanese colors.

The base is white sheeting. I've used acrylics to build up many colors. The pampas grass is of summer yarn, the flowers and crane are appliquéd, the pine embroidered.

❸❹ Put an end to war

The desire to end war is not limited to human beings. Animals, too, have this wish. I indicated clouds by using a brilliant fabric for clear rays of light. The lion's mane is unravelled linen. Colors are also applied.

❺ Bathing in sunlight

A new year has begun. Here I express the way a crane soars through the sky bathed in the first rays of sunlight. There is the fresh and bracing feeling of a new spring.

❻ Blooming in the pond

Irises are blooming in a pond. This is a flower that evokes the sense of early summer in Japan. I used shaded satin to give the feeling of light shining on the surface of the water. Movement is expressed by the quilt line.

❼❽ Blue flowers

In the fresh mist of early morning blue peonies bloom. Materials used are *kimono* fabric and satin. The centers of the flowers are embroidered.

❾ Lilies blooming in a ravine

Lilies are blooming in a ravine deep in the mountains. They are so beautiful I would like to pick them. Mountain lilies that bloom on cliffs make me think of the natural beauty of Japan.

❿ Autumn wind

Somehow I like purple flowers. They make me feel at ease. This is probably because I often see such flowers blooming naturally. When I see a Chinese bellflower blooming among the pampas grass in the garden, I feel, like many other people, that autumn has come.

⓫ Fragrant light

The peony is a flower associated with classical beauty in Japan, and it is frequently represented in Japanese paintings. There is a saying "When standing, the peony; when seated, the tree peony; when walking, the lily." The shape of this flower is thus considered to be very elegant. The white peony especially quickens my heart.

⓬⓭ Lion at play

I used dark blue cotton fabric for the base and finished the quilt with reverse appliqué and appliqué.

⓮⓯⓰ A moment in time

Time flows with a swift, swirling current. This movement is expressed by camellia flowers that mark the moment of change from the Showa to the Heisei era. Throughout the world people hope that peaceful times will continue.

⓱ Red bamboo

In Japan the four "friends" are bamboo, pine, plum and the orchid; all are auspicious. Red bamboo can be used especially for congratulatory events.

The base is *kimono* cloth. I used *haori* coat material for the appliqué, and on the reverse, silk crepe.

18 19 Advent of winter

A crane takes wing amidst trees in winter. This describes the feeling of crossing a great, cold ocean. The base is *kimono* and *haori* coat material pieced together and then quilted. The winter trees are from unevenly dyed cloth.

20 21 22 23 Floating mountains

In the distance mountains float on a sea of clouds. Sometimes they are golden, sometimes light green: sometimes they are overturned by a gloomy sky. At other times their color changes according to the color of the sky. The colors of nature cannot be described in words.

24 Poem in white

Spring flowers are as colorful as the paints on a painter's palette. But the white lotus, too, has a graceful beauty. It is often the theme in traditional Japanese paintings. I would like to depict the white lotus once through the use of paints.

25 Spring visit

Here, flower petals are not the bright color of cherry blossoms, but have changed to the color of thin India ink. I always feel great regret when I see the fallen blossoms at the end of spring.

26 27 Clear fall weather I

In Japan the chrysanthemum is the traditional autumn fragrance. Carefully tended chrysanthemums are exhibited in various places. I, too, have often gone to sketch these flowers and have enjoyed growing them. This work shows chrysanthemums blooming on an autumn evening.

The base is red sheeting. Acrylics were applied after quilting, then appliqué. I used cotton cord for the chrysanthemum flowers.

28 29 Dance poem

Flowers and folding fans are depicted. The bese is of classical colors for both Part I and Part II.

30 Six gourds

The six gourds in Japan are traditionally associated with perfect health. The base is *furoshiki* material (material traditionally used to wrap packages); the gourds are *kimono* fabric.

31 Beauties of Ukiyoe Prints

After piecing together *kimono* materials and quilting, I placed *ukiyoe* handkerchiefs about like playing cards.

32 Hero

At the annual Boys' Festival in May, warrior dolls are displayed and rice cakes wrapped in oak leaves are given as offerings. This festival is to ensure the health and strength of male children.

The base is dungaree material, appliqué on top. The mustache is painted. Indigo enlivens the frame.

33 Day of rest

During a pause in the fighting, a warrior goes to draw water. He looks as if he has temporarily forgotten the battle.

The base is quilted *obi* material of summer gauze, color applied. The warrior figure is *kimono* material and appliqué.

34 35 Flowers blooming in a secret place

Flowers bloom deep in the swamp. Black material is used for the base, colors are applied, and then appliqué. The image of the swamp is created by dyed gauze. Curtain fabric has also been dyed, threads picked out and sewed on from the top.

36 Twisted strands

This is a from series of works titled "Set free" & "Torsion" in Progressive Quilt. I want to pay attention to the way of seeing different colors and fabrics. The gray base is *kimono* material. The method is a mix of piecework and appliqué.

③⑦ Clear fall weather II

In the calm autumn breeze chrysanthemums bloom. The base is piecework, dyed gauze on top. Each thread is picked out and then appliquéd on top of layered colors.

③⑧ Wheat harvest

This work depicts pampas grass swaying in the autumn wind. The quilt line has the supporting role. The heads of the pampas grass are inserted into the quilt line without spoiling the image of the grass and then embroidered.

③⑨④⓪ Winter scene

The base is *kimono* fabric piecework. Pine, crane and narcissus etc, have been appliquéd.

④① Swamp

This work depicts a light blue banana plant blooming deep in a swamp. The base is a printed pattern. After quilting, the flowers are appliquéd.

④② Autumn prelude

Autumn on the plateau comes early. The pampas grass and other flowering plants show their autumn colors, swaying in the early autumn breeze. This scene viewed from a window of a lodge makes me feel sentimental.

④③ Up to the sky

I've always longed to be a bird flying high in the sky. I might even want wings of my own. Birds are one of my eternal themes.

④④ Building boom I

Before I knew it, buildings had sprung up one after the other. Today, again, I wondered how many people there are in those buildings.

The buildings are of wool, tweed, jersey etc. The rest of the town is from men's suit material. I used an artificial leather for the windows.

④⑤ Building boom II

When buildings in a city are illuminated, the sky color is a mixture of natural and artificial light. The base is dyed satin fabric. For the buildings I used both the front and reverse sides of men's neckties. Windows are the reverse side of necktie fabric or part of a necktie.

④⑥ Green reflection

The instant that light is released, I imagine thet there are various colors to be seen in that light. Perhaps when light is released from trees in nature, the color that we see is green. Since I wanted the quilt line to emphasize light, I boldly used both long and short lines. The base is linen dyed with vegetable dye; the green is all satin fabric.

④⑦ Seeking the light

Almost all nature's flowering plants turn their face to the ligth of the sun. Humans, plants and animals are alike in this. We live by seeking the light.

④⑧ Diverse elements broken up

The materials are linen and cotton and mixed fabrics. The base is colored yarn, then quilted and color applied.

④⑨ Emission of light

Light streams out like lightning. All the colors are mixed. The materials are mixed cotton and linen fabrics. I used satin for all the light section.

⑤⓪ Dew

Flowering plants in the rain are a beautiful green. The dew drops on a tip of a leaf are bathed in light and shine like pearls.

⑤① Meeting the unknown

When a person goes out to meet someone after

not having done so for a long time, their heart beats excitely in both anxiety and anticipation.

52 Memory of a certain day

The human memory does not work like a computer. We cannot recall memories just by pushing a button. At least my memory is like that. Somethings I remember clearly and others only come back slowly. Still others are only fragments of memories. This work depicts the human heart and mind.

53 A Play for one person only

A woman street artist frantically performs a play, but no one takes any notice. However, she hopes someone might look. Again, today, thinking of some future stage performance, she performs her one-woman play.

The base is mixed cotton and linen fabrics, the hair vinyl leather, the eyes, nose and mouth print material. The outline of the face is shown only by the quilt line.

54 Wandering protractor

Where had my protractor gone? Again today I looked everywhere. Then, one day I found many protractors, all in the same place.

55 Only one day's whim

At times I act on my whims. When stress builds up, I try to follow such caprices. After only one day of this, I can return to reality; my stress is relieved.

56 57 Singing in the rain

There's a jazz song, "Singing in the rain." A light musical. When I was small, I remember playing in puddles with my umbrella in the rain.

58 Turbulence

Suddenly the plane hit an air pocket. Everyone was frightened. There was a great commotion. The base is mixed cotton and linen fabrics. The top is satin and vinyl leather and printed fabric.

59 Light

In the evening a sudden light —— I wonder what happened? The base is colored sheeting. The light is a brilliant vinyl leather.

60 When of ladies and gentlemen meet

This work depicts the hats worn by gentlemen and ladies when they meet. The base is colored sheeting. The hats are appliqué on top of the quilting.

61 Trembling in the wind

The willow sways in the green wind. The base is colored sheeting. The willow is soft denim.

62 Drifting

Meeting in a storm, people ask for help. On top of dyed indigo cloth, I placed another piece of dyed indigo and then quilted.

63 Play

I use many flowers in my works. When I see a flower, my heart is calmed. Charmed by its beauty, sometimes I seem to forget time itself. Flowers help me feel the season and understand beauty. Here, I have tried to depict the playfulness of such flowers.

64 65 Love chorale

Flowers need butterflies and butterflies need flowers. It seems to be the same with men and women in human society. Here, I praise the love which arises from such a meeting. The centers of the flowers are embroidered.

66 Spanish fan

A gorgeous memory of passionate Spain : the Spanish flamenco dance. I have arranged in a crazy quilt a Spanish fan that remains in my memory.

67 Fantasy flower

These fantasy flowers can only be seen in dreams. The material is base cloth fabric. I inserted lining material used in Western-style clothing into chicken wire and then stitched this on from the reverse side.

p.16 ❸戦さよ終われ 　下　絵

Put an end to war　design

〝戦さよ終われ〟の制作順序

1、実物大の紙に図案を描く。

2、ベースの布にキルト線を描く。

3、バック布・キルト綿・ベースの布三枚重ねて
　しつけをかけキルトする。

4、厚紙でアップリケする山・雲・丘・馬の部分
　の型紙を作り、一つ一つに番号をふる。

5、奥になる部分から布をカットし、キルト綿を
　抱き込んでアップリケする。

6、馬の飾りの手綱はロープにキルト綿を巻き、
　布をかぶせひも状にし、編み込んだ後、縫い
　付ける。

7、ふち布は厚手の接着芯を貼り包み込み仕上げ
　る。

Directions for making
"Put an end to war"

1. Draw plan on paper of actual size.

2. Draw quilt line onto base cloth.

3. Baste together back cloth, quilt cotton and base cloth. Then quilt.

4. Make patterns from thick paper of mountain, cloud, hill and horse for appliqué. Number each one.

5. Cut the cloth from inside, work in quilt cotton and appliqué.

6. Decorative bridle for horse:-roll quilt cotton into a rope, attach to the cloth and make strands. Weave together and sew on.

7. Put thick interfacing into cloth edging, wrap up and finish.

0　　　　　　150　　　　　300 m/m

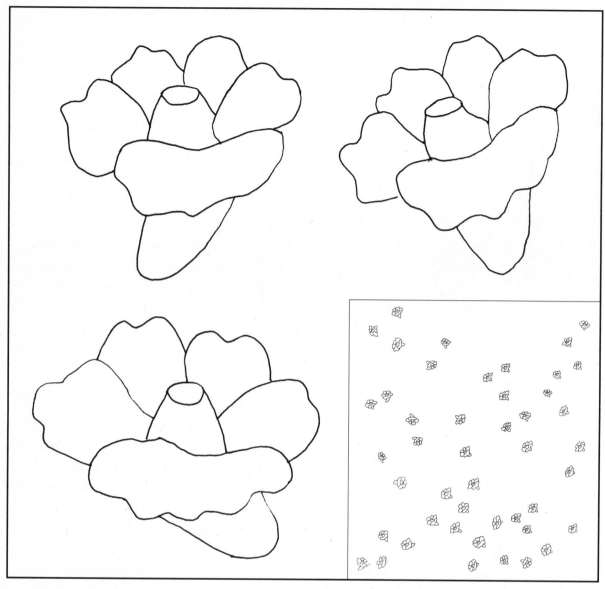

p.29　⓯時代の狭間Ⅱ　　　下　絵
A moment in time Ⅱ　design

0　　　　150　　　300 m/m

〝時代の狭間Ⅱ〟の制作順序

1、実物大の紙に図案を描く。

2、トレーシングペーパーに図案を写す。

3、厚紙で一輪ずつ型紙を作る。

4、色決めをする。

5、型紙に3mmの縫い代を付けて布を裁つ。

6、ベースをつなぎ合わせる。

7、ベースにハンドフリーでキルトラインを描き、トッ
　　プ、キルト線、裏布にしつけをかけてキルトする。

8、ベースに図案を参照しながら、ひとひらずつ綿を抱
　　き込みながらまつりつける。

9、刺繍で花芯を作る。(フレンチナッツとアウトライン
　　ステッチ)

10、ベースにカラーリングする。(7と8の間でもよい)

11、ふちを付ける。

Directions for making "A moment in time Ⅱ"

1. Draw plan on paper of actual size.

2. Transfer the plan to tracing paper.

3. Make sewing patterns of each flower from thick paper.

4. Decide on the colors.

5. Place patterns on cloth and cut out, leaving 3 mm all around for seam.

6. Attach cut-out cloth pieces to base.

7. Draw the quilt line on the base freehand. Baste together top, bottom and quilt cotton padding. Then quilt.

8. Comparing diagram to the base, work in cotton piece by piece; stitch with invisible stitch.

9. Embroider the centers of the flowers. (Outline stitch: French knots).

10. Color the base. (This may be done also between Step 7 and 8).

11. Attach edging.

あとがき

　庭先のジャカレンダの花を見ながら、久しぶりにゆっくりとティーブレイク。このカリフォルニアのブレアの自宅の回りは閑静な住宅街で、朝寝坊の私は毎朝、小鳥達のさえずりで目覚める。LAに来てから3カ月、日本と行ったり来たりの生活は、まだこれからも続くことになりそうだ。

　来年（1990）4月から5月まで、サンホゼ市にあるカリフォルニアキルトミュージアムでの個展も決まり、日本人として初めてセレクトされた事に大変感激している。エイミー女史や彼女の生徒達からも協力をしていただいた事、改めてお礼申し上げます。また、LAアートミュージアムのSANDI FOX女史からは作品について高い評価を受け、激励された。

　コンテンポラリーキルトで名高いSONYA LEE、THERESE MAY達とはシリーズで本を作っていくプランまで話し合いができた。私のジャパニーズキルトアートⅢの出版を記念して、名古屋で7月27日から開かれるキルト展に、カナダのトラディシュキルトのANNE SILVA、キルトナショナルに5年連続でセレクトされているTHERESE MAYの二人が快く出品してくれるのは、私にとって国を越えて文化の交流と友情が結ばれた事と思っている。この事は私はもちろん、生徒達にとっても喜ばしいことだと信じている。

　私が日本とアメリカと両方の国に住んでも、日本の自然が与える色の美しさは永遠に失うことはないと私は確信している。

　私のアートに対する情熱を深く理解してくれる生徒達、山本や山本の両親には言葉で表せないほど感謝しています。また、各地での個展を取材して下さったTV、マスコミの方々や愛読者の方々、アメリカでの私のマネージャの佐々木氏、光村推古書院の本田欽三社長、編集担当の上田啓一郎氏、忍海部恭子さんには誌面をお借りして厚くお礼申し上げます。

せがわ　せつこ

制作協力

日本キルトアート協会会員

（東　京）	山本詩子	八田由紀子	竹内佐輝子
（名古屋）	中島安子	宮澤道子	森田一代
	平野直子	茶納百合子	天野満紀恵
	竹内里慧子		
（大　阪）	内本敏子	野呂志保子	中野弘子
	山本孝子	岩井悦子	椿原克都子
	桑村ゆき子	山下泰子	三澤範子
	秋山洋子	小島京子	山崎静子
（広　島）	是松多鶴子	賀茂サチ子	近藤裕子
	大原素子	宮川純代	高田恵美子
	六岡京子	山下真美	梶河泰子
	新谷登紀子	大島多美子	山口利恵
	平松嘉子	熊野陽子	畑中紀代
	安原英子		

教室・連絡先 SETSUKO SEGAWA

SETSUKO SEGAWA
520 Peppertree dr Brea CA 92621 USA (714)529-7370
名古屋市千種区覚王山通り9-28-4-201
9-28-4, Kakuôzan-tori, Chikusa-ku, Nagoya, Japan.
052(752)0852　（スーザンカレッジ山本内）
052(752)0872/052(763)7535
小牧市北外山1196-4　Cat patch club 平野直子
0568(72)1047
大阪市西区新町1-33-14　新町プラザ天祥1002
06(531)9028　（木曜日）
広島市安佐南区沼田町伴700-240　是松多鶴子方
082(848)1642
福岡市中央区城内6-11　清川八寿美方
092(751)1778
宮崎市希望ケ丘1-1-1　園田みち子方
0985(56)3349
京都市中京区麩屋町通二条上ル　光村推古書院内
075(222)0361　FAX075(222)0770

せがわ せつこ プロフィール

1946年生まれ。

多摩美術大学卒業後、ヨーロッパでグラフィック、テキスタイル、インテリアディスプレイ、フラワーデザインなどを研究する。

現在日本キルトアート協会を主宰して、アメリカ、東京、大阪、名古屋、広島、福岡などで指導。又、インテリアコーディネーター、フラワーデザイナーとしても活躍している。主な著書に『キルトの世界 I 』『キルトの世界 II 』（光村推古書院刊）がある。

せがわ せつこ キルトの世界-Ⅲ
JAPANESE QUILT ART Ⅲ

平成元年8月24日発行

著　者　せがわせつこ

発行者　本田欽三

発行所　株式会社 光村推古書院

604 京都市中京区麩屋町通二条上ル
TEL　075－222－0361
FAX　075－222－0770
振替　京都6－2336

印　刷　日本写真印刷株式会社

ISBN4-8381-0103-1